CHRISTMAS AT THE RANCH

Texas Heritage Series: Number One

Christmas at the Ranch is funded in part
by the Summerfield G. Roberts Foundation.

CHRISTMAS AT THE RANCH

Elmer Kelton

Illustrated by H. C. Zachry

Foreword by Walt McDonald

MCWHINEY FOUNDATION PRESS

McMurry University

Abilene, Texas

Library of Congress Cataloging-in-Publication Data

Kelton, Elmer.
     Christmas at the ranch/Elmer Kelton; illustrated by H. C. Zachry;
       foreword by Walt McDonald.
     p. cm.—(Texas heritage series: no. 1)
     ISBN 1-893114-38-4 (cloth)
     1. Kelton, Elmer. 2. World War, 1939–1945—Personal narratives,
American. 3. Authors, American—20th century—Biography.
4. Christmas—Austria. 5. Ranch life—Texas. 6. Christmas—Texas. I. Title.
II. Series.

     PS3561.E3975Z463 2003
     813'.54—dc21   2003011663

McWhiney Foundation Press
McMurry Station, Box 637
Abilene, TX 79697-0637
(325) 793-4682
www.mcwhiney.org

Printed in the United States of America

ISBN 1-893114-38-4
10 9 8 7 6 5 4 3 2 1

Book Designed by Rosenbohm Graphic Design

Cover Designed by Stephen Jacobs, Zachry Associates

Contents

CHRISTMAS AT THE RANCH

FOREWORD

"We four Kelton boys were rich," Elmer begins this gift of a book, "because we got . . . to live on a ranch with horses and cattle and cowboys." And, he goes on to add, with family, always the best of any Christmas either on the ranch or in Austria, before or after the war. "The real pleasure of Christmas did not come from gifts anyway. It came from being with our kind, from playing with cousins George, Daisy and Ruby Gilbert, and aunt Clara Kelton."

Whether we live on a ranch or not, when we read Elmer's book, like those four Kelton boys Elmer claims were rich, so are we.

Elmer Kelton takes us to the ranch by the ear and the eye. No wonder so many of us love Elmer's stories, for we can hear and see what he means, even in the personal tales, like this history of Christmases he was lucky enough to live.

Elmer can drive and corral words where he wants them to go. He captures in one sentence the happy weeks we've spent with grandparents and the work they "let" us do. "Somehow doing chores with Daddoo was fun, whereas at home it was simply doing chores." Elmer's always a master of the perfect, folksy simile. Christmas toys "were modest by today's standards because a dollar in those Depression times looked as big as a saddle blanket."

He packs sentences with sounds that shock and jostle us along with exactly the emphasis he needs, sounds that give pleasure in and of themselves and add to the punch of what's shown. Remembering buddies in boot camp at Fort Bliss in World War II, Elmer says, "We would later sail to Europe on the same troop ship, a converted English tub so old it had a wooden hull."

"Christmas in Austria," Elmer's third story, shares a nostalgic trip in 1981 when he took his wife Ann back to her hometown, where they had met during his first Christmas there as a soldier in 1945. Swiftly, like the passing of that good time back home, Elmer takes us into charming, traditional celebrations of family and church, captured by the wit of this vintage Kelton understatement: "The Austrians know how to keep Christmas, and it is nearly Easter before they turn it loose."

Oh, yes. Elmer Kelton knows how to make Christmas and friends and family come alive, and touched by these memories in Elmer's book, it'll be a long time before we'll turn them loose.

Walt McDonald
Lubbock, Texas

CHRISTMAS AT THE RANCH

We four Kelton boys were rich. It was not because we had money, for we didn't. Money was always a short commodity in the 1930s and early 1940s. We were rich because we got to do for free what many people would have been glad to pay good money for, to live on a ranch with horses and cattle and cowboys. We spent most of our Christmases at one of two ranches: the McElroy, where our father was foreman, and the Hackamore N, which our paternal grandfather operated.

All four of us grew up on the McElroy, also known in those days as the Jigger Y. Its two hundred and twenty sections—almost a hundred and fifty thousand acres as town folks reckoned it—spread across parts of two West Texas counties, Upton and Crane. That sounds huge by Eastern standards, but in terms of productivity it was not. The land was semi-desert and required forty or fifty acres per head to keep a cow's ribs from showing through like a washboard. Average rainfall was between twelve and fifteen inches, though all too often it fell far short of the average. For that reason we always thought in terms of sections rather than acres.

A real-estate man once described a similar part of the country to me as being "sorry as hell, but pretty good." Handled properly, within its limits, it could be productive. Cattle were supposed to be scattered thinly enough not to see each other very often.

J.T. McElroy, an El Paso packing house operator, had put that ranch and several others together around the turn of the Twentieth Century to help supply his plant. It had been part of the old 1880s-1890s Quien Sabe outfit. After discovery of oil in 1925, McElroy sold the place to a French- and-American syndicate known as the Franco-Wyoming Oil Co. The new owners were far more interested in what was beneath the ground than in the grass on top. Even so, they expected the livestock operation to make its own way and pay dividends.

Despite droughts and fluctuating markets, it did pay its way
most of the thirty-six
years that Buck Kelton
was on the place, first
as a working cowboy, then as foreman and eventually as general manager.

We looked forward to rare visits by "the
French-men," the major stockholders, who
came a few times to view their property. To us
youngsters they were a curious group from some
vague land beyond the sea, dressed to the nines and
speaking a language that made us wonder how they
knew what they were saying. They may not have
known how to turn a cow down a fence, but they were
savvy when it came to the oil business and the account
books.

Dad never looked forward to Christmas with quite
the excited anticipation of us kids. For one thing, livestock did not recognize the holiday. They needed just as
much attention on Christmas as on the days before and
after. Christmas was a distraction that broke into the
ranch's orderly routine. The cowboys usually liked to
take a few days off to go back to their own homes and
celebrate with their kin, an understandable if disruptive

desire. It was left to Dad to carry the full load while they were gone. He would never spend more than one night away from home, and seldom even that.

Mother saw Christmas in a more traditional happy light. She had grown up in an Oklahoma farming and ranching home where Christmas meant a trip to church, family singing of hymns and carols, and a tree with all the trimmings, mostly homemade. Dad had grown up in a Spartan ranch atmosphere more than twenty miles north of Midland, Texas, in a time when a wagon trip to town and back took two days. His family lived far from church or organized Christmas activity. There was no Christmas tree, not even a forlorn local cedar, for a tree-less open prairie lay all around. In later years that country would produce a serious infestation of mesquite, but during Dad's boyhood a chuckwagon cook would travel far out of his way to pick up what scant firewood he could find for the next camp.

It was customary for schools and churches to set up community-type trees, but a family tree in the home was rare. It took years for Dad to reconcile himself to the notion of bringing a tree into the house. To him it was as out of place as a horse or cow would have been.

Eventually he softened to the idea of chopping down a medium-sized cedar tree on the south end of the ranch where they flourished and setting it up in the living room. He was conscious of the fire hazard, for a dry cedar could easily explode into flame. Fortunately ours never did. Nobody ever lighted real candles on it.

Mother recalled an incident early in my parents' marriage that might have had a bearing on Dad's ambivalent attitude about Christmas. Florey was a small community, now almost forgotten, near Andrews, Texas. The church there had a Christmas Eve celebration with a tree and presents. Mother's two youngest sisters, Ruth and Christine, were small girls at the time. Dad entered the church ahead of the rest of the family, carrying two Christmas-wrapped dolls under his coat. As he started to place them under the tree, one of them cried, "Mama!" The crowd laughed. Red-faced, Dad retreated to the back of the church. For years afterward he avoided both churches and Christmas trees.

In his later years, when his grandchildren were small and enthusiastically awaiting Santa Claus, he yielded to the Christmas spirit and enjoyed it as much as they did.

Often at Christmas the McElroy was deserted except for the Kelton family and any kin who might be visiting for the holidays. To us kids who had known no other place, the ranch was *home*. To the adults, home was somewhere else, and the McElroy was simply where they were currently working. The cowboys were usually bachelors. The ranch had no provision for families other than the foreman's, the windmiller's, the cook's, and that of one cowboy who held down a line camp in the sand-hills far from headquarters. The bachelor cowboys lived in an L-shaped bunkhouse which offered them small individual rooms, a lobby for loafing and socializing, and a kitchen and dining room. Most of them had a bet-ter place to be at Christmas, and usually they went.

For a long time we were the ranch's only children. In the years when Dad was foreman, the general manager was Lester S. Grant, a petroleum engineer and former professor at Colorado's School of Mines. To everybody on the ranch he was *Mister* Grant. His own children were grown and on their own. His main responsibility was the oil interests. No cowboy, he left most of the day-to-day ranching decisions to Dad. Cliff Newland took care of the windmills, but his son and daughter went to school in Midland. That left it to us Kelton boys to entertain our-selves the best—or worst—way we could. Christmas usually gave us extra playmates, cousins we rarely saw.

Though most of our Christmases were at the McElroy, some were spent at the Hackamore N north of Midland with our grandparents Bill and Daisy Kelton, known to us as Daddoo and Mammaw.

I began very early to develop an interest in Western history, and to me Daddoo was a page right out of the book. He had been born in a log house in Callahan County in 1878, soon after his parents arrived there from East Texas with a wagon and a string of horses. His father died when my grandfather was barely past ten years old, forcing him to quit school and go to work to help support his mother and five younger brothers and sisters. He broke horses and mules and cowboyed around Baird, drifting at one time as far as the famous XIT Ranch in the northern Panhandle. In 1906, when my father was about five years old, the economy became tight around Baird. Work was hard to find. Granddad's brother Frank had drifted west to Pecos and wrote home that cowboy jobs were available out there.

Daddoo decided to move his family to Pecos. But Mammaw had heard worrisome things about Pecos and said she would not consent to move any farther west than Midland. Daddoo declared that they were going to Pecos.

They went to Midland.

He was looking for cowboy work but did not find any at first, so he became a drayman, hauling freight around town until a ranch job turned up. Later he spent fifteen years as foreman of the Scharbauer Five Wells Ranch before going into partnership with Arnold

Scharbauer on a University of Texas lease known as the Hackamore N. We kids spent several happy Christmases on that place.

It was more "back to the old days" in some respects than the McElroy. That appealed to my boyish fascination with pioneer times. My grandparents had no electricity. That would come later as power lines began to be built across the rangeland. Lighting was provided by conventional kerosene lamps. In the kitchen Mammaw had an Aladdin lamp, which provided a considerably brighter light than the others. The house was of simple box-and-strip construction common in the late 1800s and early 1900s. The thin walls provided limited protection against cold winter wind. The only insulation was the wallpaper. Some of the earliest wall covering had been newspapers pasted to the wood. A closet in my grandparents' bedroom was still papered with color comic pages from about 1906. I loved to go into that closet and read the Yellow Kid and Buster Brown.

Heating came from a wood-burning kitchen range and a pot-bellied stove in the living room. We scorched ourselves on one side and froze on the other. That kept us turning like barbecue on a spit.

Indoor plumbing was to come later. Water for drinking and cooking was brought by bucket from a cistern at

the side of the house, for the ground water was strongly tinged with minerals. You had to be desperate to drink it.

A small wooden "convenience" farther out provided for other needs. A Sears or "Monkey Ward" catalog was a regular fixture. In summer we might share space with wasps which flew in through the moon-shaped cutout meant for ventilation. In winter we stayed no longer than necessary because a cold wind tended to blow in from beneath and chill our bared extremities. We "saved up" until we could no longer hold out.

By contrast, the McElroy had indoor plumbing and a thirty-two-volt Delco system which provided enough electricity for lights but very little else. And we lived only nine miles from town, compared to the more than twenty to Midland from the Hackamore N.

A two-rut road ran alongside my grandparents' yard fence but had little traffic. It was considered rude for one of the few neighbors to pass by without stopping to say howdy or at the least to honk and wave. Company was scarce. A telephone line connected the Hackamore N to the outside world. It was strung above a barbed wire fence on staves which raised it up to about the level of a man on horseback. A cowboy could ride along and patch the line without getting down from his horse. Mammaw kept up with the news by listening in on the party line. Sometimes she would break in and contribute to the conversation. Everybody did it in those days. If you wanted to keep a secret, you did not mention it on the telephone.

On the west side of the ranch house a set of outside stairs led up to a cramped attic room which Daddoo called "the chute." We boys often slept there on pallets near the warm chimney that came up from beneath. In summer we were more likely to sleep on pallets on the porch or out in the yard.

Because there were always little ones who still had faith in Santa Claus, we got up on Christmas morning to see what gifts had been left during the night. The toys were modest by today's standards because a dollar in those Depression times looked as big as a saddle blanket. But we were conditioned not to expect too much and to take pleasure in whatever we received. The stockings we had hung up the night before usually contained an apple or orange, candies and a handful of pecans, Brazil nuts or whatever our folks had managed to find in town. Always a reader, I was happy if I found a Big Little Book or two with my name on them. I preferred the movie tie-in kind with stills from Western stars like Ken Maynard or Buck Jones.

The real pleasure in Christmas did not come from gifts anyway. It came from being with our kin, from playing with cousins George, Daisy and Ruby Gilbert, and aunt Clara Kelton, who was the baby of her family and in the same general age bracket as the rest of us. If the weather was pleasant we played outdoors. If it was not, we stayed inside and played board games like Monopoly and made a lot of noise that no doubt was a distraction to the adults.

Ranch chores did not take a holiday. On a few lucky occasions Daddoo let us go with him when he fed his cattle. He never owned a pickup. He did his ranch work on horseback or in a team-drawn wagon. He had an old sheet-metal feed barn that had turned reddish with rust over the years. The standard feed supplement in those days was pelleted cottonseed cake, forty-one percent protein, bought in hundred-pound sacks that none of us were strong enough to lift. I always liked the taste of it, though the grit was hard on teeth. The pellets were good ammunition for throwing at one another. They didn't hurt as much as a rock.

Daddoo would bring his wagon up beside a loading dock. He dragged the sacks out one at a time and emptied them into a wooden box beneath the wagon seat. As he came upon his cattle—they usually trotted to meet him, bawling with every step—he would shovel the pellets out to them with a small hand scoop. One cow, one scoopful.

I remember a couple of times that he let my brother Myrle and me go with him to pick up dead mesquite limbs for firewood. Daddoo had a large black birthmark on the back of his neck. On one occasion a wagon wheel dropped into a hole and shook loose a large stick that fell and struck the birthmark. He doubled over in pain. We youngsters had no inkling that the birthmark was a melanoma which would eventually kill him.

Myrle put an end to our wood-gathering expeditions. While Daddoo and I picked up dry limbs, Myrle was given the responsibility of holding the reins. Daddoo was cautious enough to make certain he did it from the ground, not from the wagon seat. Something spooked the team. They jerked the reins from Myrle's small hands and stampeded back toward the house. Entering the yard, they hubbed a gatepost and made kindling out of the wagon.

Christmas dinner was always a highlight, whether at the Hackamore N or at the McElroy. Mammaw kept turkeys in a small enclosure behind the house. Turkeys were never the smartest members of the bird kingdom. The slightest unfamiliar noise sent them into a gobbling frenzy. They consumed every blade of grass, every emerging weed, leaving the pen as slick as a peeled onion. One of them paid the price each Christmas and wound up on the dinner table, surrounded by dressing, biscuits, gravy and a variety of pies, cakes and fruit salad, not to mention the ranch staple, red beans.

Mammaw knew how to make red beans taste almost like dessert. During the years Daddoo was a ranch foreman, Mammaw was the unofficial and unpaid cook for however many cowboys happened to be around on a given day. Red beans and biscuits were the culinary foundation of ranch life.

Going home was always something of a letdown for us kids, though it was probably a relief to our elders. An old story in our family tells of a great-grandmother who waved goodbye to kinfolks as they rode away in their wagon after an extended visit. She said, "They blessed me twice—once when they came and again when they left."

The trip home involved driving seventy-five or eighty miles, part of it over rough two-rut roads whose high centers could hang up a car. In rainy weather they could deteriorate into bottomless holes of mud that would bog a car to the hubs. When Dad was driving, such occasions could introduce us to a new and pungent vocabulary that we never learned in school or in church. The Christmas glow seldom lasted all the way home, for we knew that Dad had plenty of chores in mind to make up for time lost at the Hackamore N.

Perhaps because going to our grandparents' house involved a change of scenery and a sense of roughing it in relative comfort, Christmases at home on the Jigger Y never quite raised us to the same pitch of enjoyment. For one thing they did not excuse us from our daily chores. Those went on as usual and sometimes increased because the cowboys were absent. Somehow doing

chores with Daddoo was fun, whereas at home it was simply doing chores.

Christmas at home was simple and unstructured but had a special glow all its own. The gifts were modest. Probably the greatest gift I received in those days was a cowboy suit when I was seven or eight. Mother made a pair of imitation chaps out of brown oilcloth for me.

They looked like the ones Dad and the cowboys wore when working cattle in the brush except that these offered little defense against mesquite thorns. I probably received a cap pistol too, but mainly I remember the chaps. I already had boots. I had worn boots as far back as I could remember. I was probably ten or twelve years old before I ever had a pair of regular shoes like the town boys wore.

What toys we received were usually bought with a view toward durability. We improvised a lot. When the weather was good we built miniature corrals out of matchsticks and twigs on the south side of our house. Multi-colored marbles became horses and cattle. In those days most of the real cattle came in a minimum of colors: red and white for Herefords, pure black for Angus. In more recent times crossbreeding has produced cattle of all colors, reminding me of those rainbow marbles.

Sometimes we lucked onto a large cardboard packing box. It became a wagon, though without wheels. One boy would get into the box and let the others push him around the ranch's large yard. The screeching sound made by that box sliding across the gravel was not unlike a piece of chalk dragged across a blackboard. Mister Grant, the manager, found it a nuisance, as did his city-raised wife who hated every day she ever lived on that isolated ranch. One Christmas, just before he left on a holiday trip to Colorado, Mister Grant brought us a bright red Jumbo wagon and said he hoped we never again would push each other around in a cardboard box.

That red wagon lasted for years.

The Newlands lived next door to us in a sprawling old ranchhouse originally built by J. T. McElroy for his use when he visited the ranch. He would ride the T&P train as far as Odessa, then rent a hack and drive out to the ranch, the oldtimers told us. On one such trip he stopped by the Dawson windmills to water his team and found a couple of his cowboys there roping cattle for the fun of it. Neither of them knew him. He asked, "Don't you think the owner of those cattle would object to you mistreating them?"

One of the cowboys said, "He's a rich old so-and-so who lives in El Paso. He'll never know."

McElroy drove on down to headquarters and had the cowboys' checks ready when they rode in. He told them, "That rich old so-and-so from El Paso says you're fired."

Cliff Newland was responsible for keeping more than seventy windmills running. That was a steady chore when the old Eclipse types had to be greased at least a couple of times a week. Those were gradually replaced by self-oiling Aermotor steel mills, which allowed Cliff more leisure time. He spent much of it exploring nearby Castle Gap, on the old stagecoach and immigrant trail which led to Horsehead Crossing. Legend said a stolen shipment of gold had been buried in the gap and never recovered. That gold became an obsession with Cliff. He dug holes all over the gap hunting for it. It was probably just as well that he never found it, for the search gave a special meaning to his life. It is said that the journey is sometimes more important than the destination. The search and the hope kept him going into his nineties.

The ranch had a Norwegian resident bookkeeper named Tom Schreiner. He had come over from the old country as a young man to seek his fortune. He never found his own, but he helped others in the making of theirs. Christmas is a family time, and he had no family of his own. The holidays must have been an especially lonely, melancholy time for him, for he usually sought solace in drink. In effect, he was in exile on this dusty West Texas ranch far from the company's main offices in California, supposedly because of his drinking.

Though he lived there and was part of the ranch's extended family, he remained essentially a loner, some-times pacing the long porch of the office or the short porch of a small frame house which had been allotted to him. He was an intelligent, well-educated man and had had a wealth of experience in exotic places like Norway and New York, New Orleans and California. Our world was pretty well enclosed by a barbed wire fence, where-as his had no bounds except those he imposed upon himself. He frequently drove to town on weekends and immersed his sorrows in a glass.

His antics amused us sometimes, though there was always a sadness about them, a regret for such a warm and talented man who was wasting himself this way. I especially remember one Sunday afternoon when he came walking in from the town road, looking to Dad for help. He had run his coupe into the ditch a mile or so from headquarters. He explained that he had started walking with a six-pack of beer. Accountant that he was, he mentally calculated how far each beer would have to last.

"And, Buck," he said, "I just missed it by a hundred yards."

One Christmas we boys had been given a basketball. We were dribbling it across the yard when Mister Schreiner came out onto the porch of the ranch office, obviously somewhat worse for wear. He veered over to us and took the ball. He said, "Venn I vass a boy, I vass very good at baseball," whereupon he kicked the basketball into a cultivated cactus patch. It expired like a punctured balloon.

He often talked wistfully of "the old country." It was long his dream to return there when he retired and spend his last years among family and boyhood friends. After World War II he finally managed to make the move back to Norway. But by then he was old and unwell. The land of his memories was a bitter disappointment. It had changed much during his long years in America. The friends of his youth were dead or aging as he was. His kin did not know him. He began writing letters back to his American friends, expressing a longing to return to Texas as soon as his health improved. It never did. He died, as alone as ever, in a land that was no longer home.

Even his dreams had abandoned him.

Sadness occasionally tinged our Christmases too. Once I went with Mother to the funeral of a young cousin who had died on Christmas Eve after a long illness. It was one of those dull gray, dusty winter days when a dry norther's cold wind seemed to moan a dirge through the trees, through the telephone lines, under the eaves. Even now, I dread that kind of day, for it reawakens the melancholy feeling of that most sad of funerals.

My brother Bill always seemed accident-prone, mainly around horses but occasionally in other ways as well. He held onto a Christmas "baby giant" firecracker too long and split his thumb. Once in a visit to the Hackamore N he toddled around behind a horse and was kicked in the stomach. He nearly died. Some years later he hung a foot in a stirrup and was almost dragged to death.

My youngest brother, Gene, was nicknamed Boob after a comic strip character of the time, Boob McNutt. One frigid Christmas he walked out onto ice that had formed across a big surface tank. The ice was thin, and he fell through. Myrle was there; they had been playing on the tank dam. He broke ice all the way out to where Gene was floundering and rescued him. By the time he carried him to the house, their wet clothes had frozen stiff.

Justice would have called for him to be hailed as a hero for saving his younger brother. But no, he was spanked for letting Gene walk out onto the ice in the first place. As someone has said, no good deed goes unpunished.

The joy of Christmas seems always to be followed by a letdown when it is over. All too quickly we reverted to routine. We caught up on chores that might have been short-changed, like chopping a supply of wood for the stoves. Dad, on the other hand, usually seemed relieved. He had been brought up in the old school which dictated that you saw to your animals before your own needs and wants. His first priority was the horses, second the cattle, third the rest of us. In later years he mellowed as his grandchildren came along. Through them he vicariously enjoyed Christmas in a way he never could when he was younger and burdened by responsibilities that sometimes seemed too heavy to carry.

My grandparents left the Hackamore N shortly after the outbreak of World War II and moved in to Midland. The adults knew but did not tell us youngsters that Daddoo was terminally ill from his melanoma. I saw the old place just twice after that. A few years after the war I visited an aunt and uncle who were living there. Somehow the place had shrunk. It was much smaller than I remembered.

Then, not many years ago, I was traveling along a graded road east of Andrews and north of Midland. Suddenly I got the feeling that a windmill I saw looked familiar. I followed a two-rut road to it and then a little beyond. There, to my surprise, was the old Hackamore N headquarters. I had entered it from the back side on a road that had not existed in my boyhood. The current cowboy was living in a mobile home. The old ranch house was in the process of being torn down. Most of it was on the ground, but part of the stairway up to the chute was still standing. So were the walls of the closet in what had been my grandparents' bedroom. The old comics I had loved as a kid were no longer there.

I walked out to the surface tank where we used to swim in the summer. There I found the remains of Daddoo's old wagon. Its bed sat flat on the ground, its wheels lying off to the side. I left, for I did not want the modern reality to intrude on my memories of a magic place.

The McElroy Ranch was sold in 1965. The headquarters, showing their age, were abandoned in favor of a newer set of facilities farther south. I recently visited the place. No one lives there now. Cattle roamed the big ranch yard that we had worked hard to keep neat and clean. The L-shaped bunkhouse and the old Newland home were gone. The barn, the office, the little Schreiner house were in final stages of ruin. Only our family house would still be livable, and it would require a lot of work.

I did not stay there any longer than I had stayed at the Hackamore N. I prefer to see the place in my mind as it used to be and relive in memory the joyful Christmases the Kelton family spent there when the world seemed young.

THE BEST CHRISTMAS

In the opening of Charles Dickens' *A Tale of Two Cities*, he wrote that it was the best of times and the worst of times. Looking back over a lifetime of pleasant Christmases, I sometimes think the best I ever had was probably in 1944. It was also the worst, for some of the same reasons that it was the best.

World War II was in its third year for the United States before I turned eighteen and received my call to service. Many of my close friends from our old high school in Crane, Texas, were a bit older and had already gone into uniform. I suffered guilt and delusions of inferiority because I was finishing my second year in college, yet was not old enough to shoulder my share of the burden. But in April, 1944, President Roosevelt sent me his greetings almost before my younger brothers had eaten all of my birthday cake. I had tried to enlist in the Navy at seventeen but was turned down because I had flat feet. The Army willingly accepted me, however. I eventually wound up in the walking infantry, which has left me distrustful of the military mind ever since. But that is another story.

I had never had a Christmas away from family. I did not look forward to Christmas of 1944.

My induction was at Fort Bliss in El Paso, then an important training ground for anti-aircraft. I was assigned to A Battery of the 56th Batallion for basic training. I found myself thrown into the company of hundreds of young men from all over the United States as well as Mexico. The Army was accepting a great many young Mexican nationals. They were promised they would earn American citizenship for their service. Many did not speak English, and what some of the Yankee and deep-South sergeants could do to Spanish names bordered on the criminal. It was also hilarious. At one roll call the sergeant stumbled over several but had muddled his way through until he read, "Ga-WILL- ermo TRUDGE-illo." Nobody answered, but someone should have, for the count was right. Again, much louder and redder in the face, he shouted, "Ga-WILL-ermo TRUDGE-illo." Finally someone realized what he was trying to say and nudged Guillermo Trujillo, who shouted, "Here!" The sergeant gave him a look that said a week on KP and demanded, "Why don't you answer when you hear your name?"

I made a lot of temporary friends in that outfit, though at the time I didn't know how temporary they would be. We shared a set of five-man tarpaper shacks on the eastern edge of the post, near the Air Corps runways. I still remember the names, like Ralph Howery of Indiana, Hubert Langley of Arkansas, Jimmy Knapil of Ohio. We were a diverse and cosmopolitan group, a cross-section of America.

And I remember Lee Irvine, a small, quiet fellow who turned out to be the only ranch-raised boy in the outfit besides myself. He came from Buffalo, Wyoming, which sounded like a romantic Old West place to a kid from the Crane County sandhills. At the lower end of our battery area were cavalry stables which had only recently been deactivated. They still smelled of horses and hay. Nights, once in a while, I would get homesick and stray off down there to lean on the fence and sniff a little scent of home. More than once I found Lee Irvine there, doing the same thing. He was homesick, too.

Our battery commander was a tough little rooster of a first lieutenant named Mergen, barrel-chested, possessed of a deep bass voice much like that of Eugene Pallette, the grand character actor of the 1930s and 1940s. With three words he could peel the hide from a recruit at a hundred yards. A top sergeant in the regular army before the war, he had a wartime commission but still was a top sergeant at heart. He was utterly without mercy, constantly driving, never pleased with anything we did, always demanding more than the human body could stand. I considered him the meanest man I had ever known, a view shared by every buck private in the outfit. Always, seemingly every time we turned around, Mergen was there, threatening, bullying, cursing.

I began to suspect that all was not as he made it seem, however. Through the Red Cross I received word that my grandfather was dying in Midland after a long struggle with a melanoma. Though army custom was that enlisted men were granted emergency leaves only for deaths in the immediate family—father, mother, siblings, wife—a sympathetic Mergen provided me a pass that got me to Midland just an hour before my grandfather died.

Christmas had always been a family time for us, and I was sure I would spend this one in a military camp scrubbing out garbage cans, not an infrequent assignment for me at Bliss. But we finished our basic training late in December, and to our pleasant surprise we were all furloughed home for the holidays. By that time the German air force, the Luftwaffe, was all but destroyed, and the Army didn't need any more anti-aircraft personnel. I was ordered to report after Christmas to Camp Howze near Gainesville, Texas, for crash training in the infantry. I would be in Europe by February or March, they said, ready for front-line combat.

As we lined up to receive our individual orders, there stood the lieutenant, the monster Mergen, his eyes shining with tears. He told us something he had felt he could not tell us before: he had already been to hell and back. He knew what combat was. He had purposely made life as hard as possible for us, knowing he could never make it as hard as what some of us might be going to. He had toughened us as much as he knew how, hoping he might enable us to survive. With tears on his cheeks he asked God's blessing on us, then saluted, turned around and walked away without looking back.

It is a sad thing about wartime military life that you make friends, then lose contact with them as you are scattered in all directions. We all promised to write to one another, but most of us never did. Of all the friends with whom I stood that final afternoon on the Fort Bliss parade ground, the only one I ever saw or heard from again was Lee Irvine, the ranch boy from Wyoming. We would later sail to Europe on the same troop ship, a converted English tub so old it had a wooden hull.

The lieutenant's words, but even more the look in his face and eyes, rode the bus home with me to what by then I feared might be my last Christmas. A dark premonition began to build, one that would not leave me until my part of the war was over. I believe every combat soldier has it, but each thinks his is the only one.

Up to that point it was a Christmas like most of my seventeen others, spent quietly on the McElroy Ranch where my father had been foreman for most of a dozen years. I hung up my uniform and put on my Levis and boots. I rode horseback and cowboyed a little, though I had never been very good at it. I had always suspected I was a disappointment to my cowboy father. My youngest brother at twelve was a better hand than I was at eighteen.

For a few days, out of uniform, I tried to put aside the dread that by now lay like a cold lump of lead in the pit of my stomach, a dread I dared not talk about to anyone, least of all my mother and father. I made up my mind that if it was to be my last Christmas, I wanted to make it my best. I gloried in the familiar faces and stored up memories that I hoped would carry me through.

In that respect it was very possibly the best Christmas I ever had, and the greatest gift was those few short days of peace and love in the only totally sane place I had ever found: home. And it was the worst, for that dread never went away. Always in an unguarded moment, in response to something someone said or a worried look I could see in someone's eyes, I would feel that chill.

It seemed a short Christmas. Almost before I realized it, I had to go to Odessa to catch the bus. There was something melancholy about bus stations in those wartime years . . . I had the same feeling about airports during the long Vietnam tragedy much later on. They were sad places, places where men too young said goodbye to wives and sweethearts and mothers and went off into a dark unknown from which they might not return.

A few years after World War II a memorial plaque I saw on a wall near the bus station in San Antonio said it all. The words as I recall were, "A few feet from this spot, a loving father said goodbye to his beloved son for the last time on this earth."

I boarded my bus with a sack of fruitcake and cookies and a stomach so cold I could not eat them. My best Christmas was over.

Camp Howze was a miserable place of hastily-constructed tarpaper barracks and cold, wet winds, of coal-fired heaters and deep black mud. Gainesville was something else, however. In the downtown Methodist Church on the two or three Sundays I was able to leave the post, the people treated me with a kindness and warmth that has remained with me all these years. They gave me a prayer book that I carried with me overseas and that I still hold among my treasures. They did not take away the dread, but they gave me strength to live with it.

I made new friends at Howze, not one of whose names I can remember. The only old friend I found there was Lee Irvine. He was assigned to a different unit, but we crossed trails a few times.

After a perfunctory training session of about six or seven weeks they loaded us on troop trains, hauled us to Camp Kilmer, New Jersey, put us on troop ships and rushed us to Germany for the final stage of the European war. As always, I lost track of everyone I knew. I joined a 26th Division infantry company as a replacement the night of the Rhine River crossing. We went over in a truck convoy on a pontoon bridge the

Army engineers had constructed during the day under constant enemy fire.

The worst of the war was already over. Despite all my forebodings, my personal combat experience was far less dreadful than I had feared. The Germans were in full retreat. Much of the time we were ordered to ride atop Sherman tanks in the interests of speed. It was one of these tanks that took me out of the war a couple of weeks before the German surrender. It ran into a stone wall and pinned my foot, making confetti of my boot and a mess of my ankle.

I developed some idea of the enormity of the war when I watched refugees and concentration-camp survivors by the hundreds lining the roads, going somewhere, anywhere, to get away from where they had been. It was even more forcefully driven home to me on Memorial Day. I was on crutches in an Army hospital outside of Paris. Those of us able to move around were offered a bus ride out to a military cemetery for services. I remember that some officers spoke, but I do not remember anything they said. What I remember was the feeling of awe and sadness as I looked at row upon row of Christian crosses and Stars of David, thousands of them stretching all the way up a gentle hillside and beyond. And flying over them, lifting and falling in a gentle wind, was the American flag. That scene has come back to me a thousand times when I look up at the stars and stripes and think of all those men—most of them young like I was—who gave all there was to give for their country.

I was a late arrival, so I was obliged to stay for a little more than a year after the war in Europe had ended. I spent the Christmas of 1945 in Austria, with the family of a young woman who was to become my wife and whose lingering accent and phonetic spelling were to provide amusement to our children and grandchildren for years to come. It was a long way from home, and the holiday customs were in many ways different from those I had known, but it has always remained a standout Christmas for me, as 1944 has always been.

In the first years after coming home I sent Christmas cards to some of my old army friends, or tried to. Most of the cards came back undelivered. Often I would wonder about this one or that one and what had ever become of him. Among others, I wondered about the boy from Wyoming.

In my later career as a livestock journalist I sometimes found myself in the company of stockmen from other parts of the country. Several times I met ranch people from Wyoming. I would always ask if they had ever heard of Lee Irvine. Always I drew a blank.

It was thirty years after the war when one day at the office of the *Livestock Weekly* I received a letter from Van Irvine of Casper, Wyoming, inquiring about advertising rates. He wanted to auction off a big band of sheep. I answered his query and at the end of the letter casually asked him if he might be kin to my Wyoming friend of Fort Bliss days.

A few days later I received his reply. Lee Irvine had been his kid brother, he said. He was killed in April, 1945, a few days after arrival in Germany.

Thirty years fell away in an instant, and the feeling of grief was as strong as if the loss had just happened. I just sat there awhile, frozen.

I have had almost sixty Christmases since 1944. But it was the last for Lee Irvine, and for others I knew. It was the last Christmas in which the world seemed young.

It was in some ways the best Christmas I ever had. It was also my worst.

"The Best Christmas" was first published in *Texas and Christmas*, TCU Press, 1983.

CHRISTMAS IN AUSTRIA

Austria is the birthplace of that most sacred of Christmas carols, *Silent Night*, said to have been composed for the guitar after a church organ broke down. As a soldier I spent the Christmas of 1945 there in a magnificent mountain-and-lake region of the Alps known as the Salzkammergut, which literally translated means "good chamber of salt." Salt was mined there as early as Roman times. It is still mined today, as are the foreign tourists, mostly German and English.

Though it was my first Christmas away from my own family in Texas, I was fortunate in having become acquainted with a family in Ebensee, where I was stationed, and most especially with the young woman who would later become my wife and life partner for these last fifty-six years. She was known as Anni in the old country. The name was simplified to Ann when she came to Texas.

That Christmas in 1945 was a frugal one. The war had left Austria badly battered and on its knees economically. The Lipp family (pronounced *Leep*) like the rest was making do with very little and could not provide much for the holiday beyond good wishes. Strict rationing limited the food supply to a subsistence level. Stores had little to sell, and citizens had little money to buy with. But they were thankful the war was over, and with it domination by Nazi Germany that had begun when Hitler grabbed the country in 1938.

I managed to get a bottle of illegal cognac out of the enlisted men's club and present it to my future father-in-law, pleasing him very much. Outside, the snow was deep and the weather cold. But inside, the cheery Christmas feeling was much like the one I had known at home. Among other things I learned the German words to *Silent Night*, or *Stille Nacht*. For me it is *the* Christmas carol.

Alois Lipp had been a soldier for the Austro-Hungarian empire in World War I. A woodsman by inclination, he worked in an Ebensee factory and was a cobbler on the side, though by the time I knew him he had retired. He was a small man with a gleam of gentle mischief shining in his eyes. He sported a generous handlebar moustache that turned up at the ends. He enjoyed his wine when he could get it, though for a time after the war it was hard to come by. After a few drinks he liked to sing regardless of time or place. When he serenaded the neighbors while walking home from the tavern, Frau Lipp sometimes moved well ahead of him, hoping nobody would realize they belonged together.

She loved socializing and kept up to the minute on the community gossip. I have wondered sometimes how she handled the gossip when I—an American soldier—began being seen with her youngest daughter.

By Christmas Ann and I had an understanding. I had picked up enough G.I. German to get by on, but I worked extra hard to learn how to tell her father that I loved her and wanted to marry her. He listened patiently to my presentation, shrugged and said, "Take her." I don't think he actually believed that I would.

Military restrictions made it impossible for us to marry at the time. I was accepted as more or less a member of the family despite doubts among many that our courtship would last beyond my stay in Europe. Soldiers were notorious for short-term romances. I had to return home and become a civilian to get around the military red tape. It was 1947 before I could get Ann into this country and stand with her in front of the minister.

Later on, my father-in-law commented that he could not understand why most of his daughters married "foreigners." Mitz married an Italian, Anni married an American, Resi married a Viennese, and Laura married a man who lived about three miles around the lake in the village of Traunkirchen. Only Frieda married what he considered a hometown boy.

The years went by. Ann became an American citizen and adapted to just about everything American except perhaps our Texas summer heat. But each December as the holidays approached she would comment, "Somehow it doesn't seem quite like Christmas." She would remember Christmases back in prewar Austria and wonder aloud if they were still the same as they used to be.

She kept in contact with a friend from her hometown who was living in a Chicago suburb. The friend, Traudl Barts, made a trip back to Ebensee one Christmas. On her return she told Ann, "It's not the same as it used to be. It's better."

In 1981 I decided to give Ann a special Christmas gift, a trip back to her old home over the holidays so she could see for herself if it really was better. At first she was a little reluctant because that would mean spending Christmas away from our own family. Our sons and daughter by then were grown and on their own. But the idea began to grow on her and she became excited at the prospect.

We had gone back to Austria only twice at that time, once in 1954 and again in 1976. Her parents had passed away during that twenty-two year span, but she still had sisters and a brother as well as many nieces and nephews. We had hosted her sister Resi and brother-in-law Karl Redl in Texas in 1975 and stayed in their home during our 1976 visit.

So we celebrated our family Christmas at home in early December and then made the trip. Our daughter Kathy went with us to see her mother's homeland and meet cousins she had never seen. Our own celebrations had little structure or routine. We usually put up the Christmas tree and decorations sometime after Thanksgiving and bought presents as the opportunity and the mood struck us. We had Christmas dinner, handed out the presents, and that was about it.

The Austrian Christmas was much more structured, with traditional observances to be made on specific days. Like many towns in that country, Ebensee had a tradition of making and displaying elaborate nativity scenes, known as *Krippen*, in the home and in the church. In the Lipp family many of the hand-carved nativity pieces had been passed down for generations, additions being made and displays enlarged as the years went by. Ann's nephew Fredi devoted the major part of one room to a huge layout that must have numbered well over a hundred pieces. There was a definite schedule for placing them. The Christ Child did not go into the scene until Christmas, at which time the other human figures were turned to face Him. The Three Wise Men did not appear until January 6, long after most American homes would have put away all the pieces.

On Sunday it was customary that many people open their homes for visitors to view the *Krippen*. Some of these were far larger even than Fredi's and attracted spectators from all over. Many of the oldest were an incongruous mixture of familiar Austrian scenes and the makers' quaint notions of what a village in Bethlehem must look like, palm trees mingled with pines, desert sands with Alpine mountains, the crude stable standing amid multi-story houses of the old German style.

One of the most popular was in a farmhouse far out at the edge of town. A Lipp family procession trudged

through deep snow to see it. Healing after having bro-
ken a leg, Ann's brother Louis was walking on a cane.
The trip was an ordeal for him because his cane kept
driving down into the snow, like a scene from Chaplin's
The Gold Rush. The cold got through to a steel pin in his
leg and caused him considerable pain. But Louis had a
stubborn streak—a notorious family trait—and would
not turn back. On the return we finally persuaded him
to accept a ride in a passing truck. He got off at a
gasthaus, ordered a beer and waited for us.

That stubborn streak got Louis into and out of trou-
ble several times. He was an electrician by trade. During
World War II the Nazis set up a forced-labor camp near
a quarry on the outskirts of town. It was not officially a
death camp in the sense of Auschwitz, but the inmates
were poorly fed, clothed and housed, and they were so
brutally overworked that during the war great numbers
died of mistreatment.

Austrians were subject to draft into the German
army. Louis was deferred because of his work. He was
on a job where a couple of emaciated inmates from the
prison camp were working under an SS guard. They
were literally starving to death. When the officer was
not looking, Louis would slip them his meager lunch.
One day the officer caught him at it. Flying into a rage,

he declared that if it happened again he would shoot one of the prisoners and put Louis in his place. When angered, Louis was not given to worrying much about consequences. He happened to be working with a blow torch. As the officer turned his back, Louis applied the flame where he thought it would leave the most lasting impression. Within days he found himself an unwilling member of the German army.

As the war neared its end, he and several other Austrian soldiers were stationed in Czechoslovakia. They could read the handwriting on the wall. Half a dozen of them decided it was time to go home rather than be killed in the last days of the war, serving an army they had been forced into and a cause they detested. Deserting, they set out afoot, walking by night, hiding by day, crossing over the line into Austria. One by one they peeled off in their own directions. Most made it to their destinations uncaught, though one unfortunate was captured at the door of his own home and summarily shot in front of his family.

Finally it was down to Louis and one friend. Walking alongside a railroad track in the dark, they saw a train coming and decided to grab hold and ride awhile. The friend was long-legged and managed to swing up onto the side of a car. Louis was slower. He could not catch the train. It disappeared into the night, and he was left there by himself to complete his long journey alone. He finally managed to reach Ebensee, but it was a long time before his friend made it home. As it turned out, the train was carrying German troops to the Russian front. The friend almost died in a miserable Russian prisoner of war camp.

Louis worked his way home over the mountains, entering Ebensee from the back side and hoping he could make it to his house unseen. But by the time he reached there American soldiers had occupied the town. He ran into an unexpected G.I. roadblock. By this time he had ditched his telltale uniform in favor of clothes liberated from a wash line, but he still wore his army boots. He hoped the soldier would not recognize them for what they were. Despite a language barrier, Louis managed to convey the fiction that he was a forester. He had been working in the woods and had left his identification at home so he would not lose it. The soldier sent him on his way. He had a joyous reunion with his family but remained hidden for several days until he decided the Americans were benign and turned himself in. To his surprise they gave him a paying job and put him to work.

Ann's other brother, Martin, had been a member of an anti-Nazi youth group. After Germany took the country he was thrown into a concentration camp for a time, then placed in the army. He survived the war but died relatively young.

The Lipp family followed old Catholic traditions in observing Christmas. Advent inaugurated the season four Sundays before the holiday. A new candle was ceremoniously lighted on each Sunday.

The family Christmas tree did not go up until Christmas Eve, but it stayed in place until early February. It was kept in an unheated room so it did not dry out prematurely. They lighted real candles on it, which we never did at home because a dried-out tree would be a fire hazard. The Lipps were a working family and never could afford a fancy Christmas. When Ann was a girl, before the war, her mother would often steal away her doll, put new clothes on it—homemade of course—and wrap it up as a new gift.

Ann's father would take the children to church for the six o'clock mass, followed by a procession to the cemetery to light candles on family graves. During their absence her mother would put up the tree and place beneath it whatever gifts they had. Besides traditional ornaments reused every year, the tree would be decorated with cookies and candies. Ann and her next oldest sister ate these from the lower part of the tree when the parents were not looking and let the blame fall on the family's little dog.

After a modest meatless supper, carols would be sung and the Lord's Prayer recited for the sick and the departed members of the family. The entire prayer would be spoken for each one.

Ann said her mother could think of relatives she had never even heard of. The prayers went on and on while the children helplessly stared at the gifts, itching to get into them. Not until the last prayer was said were they given the go-ahead. Finally there would be a midnight supper and the sound of carols played from the tower of the church.

On our visit we soon found that Traudl had been right about Christmas there being better than it used to be. Economically almost everyone was far better off than during the postwar holiday I had spent there in 1945. Decorations were brighter and more elaborate but retained a strong religious flavor. The Austrians had their own version of Santa Claus, Saint Nikolaus, but the Christ Child was still the centerpiece of Christmas observances. Though commercialism had crept in, it was modest compared to what we encountered at home. The larger towns and cities had their festive *Kristkindl* markets which sold all sorts of holiday goods and gifts, but the name still paid homage to the one whose birthday it was.

Saint Nikolaus was kindly, like Santa Claus, but naughty children were threatened with a visit from Krampus, a dark and forbidding horned figure who accompanied Nikolaus on the night of December 5, walking the streets and pathways dragging a chain and carrying switches with which he threatened to punish the wayward young.

Ann's mother, who had led the Christmas observances at home, had passed away in 1960. Louis's wife Nanni inherited the matriarchal duties for her branch of the family. We followed the old tradition of going in a body to six o'clock mass while Nanni remained behind to take care of tree and trimmings. After the mass we joined a procession and walked several blocks to the cemetery. By then it was pitch dark and quite cold. The cemetery was in several tiers on a mountainside. We stopped at the entrance and bought candles. These were placed and lighted on all the family graves. I climbed up to the top tier and looked down. I have seen few scenes in my life that moved me as much as that sea of flickering candles, the people kneeling in prayer while a brass band played traditional Christmas music.

Afterward, as per custom, we returned to Louis's house. The tree was ready. Ann's nephew Fredi had a son of his own by this time, about five years old. Watching him while Nanni went through the long ritual of prayers for the departed, I remembered what Ann had said about her own mother. I thought little Fredi was in some danger of nervous collapse by the time Nanni went through all the dead relatives, not to mention many live ones.

Most homes in Austria accommodate multiple families. In this case there were three, living on three floors of a house whose beams had dates carved into them going back to the 1500s. It was custom to go to each floor and admire each family's tree and the gifts that had been exchanged. There were toasts to make and carols to be played and sung. Louis's family was musically inclined, each male member playing some kind of instrument, so they performed awhile on every floor. Finally, at midnight, they enjoyed a festive late supper of sauerkraut, sausage and whatever else was at hand.

Louis opened the windows so we could hear a brass quintet playing carols in the church tower, as they had done much longer than anyone living could remember. The cold night air carried the sound with crystal clarity across the town, echoing it back from the mountainsides.

Even after Christmas the observances continued. There was no dancing from November 25 until the end of December. Saint Katharine's Day on New Year's Eve inaugurated a series of dances that would continue until Lent. Beginning with the church's six p.m. prayer bell, groups of singers marched from house to house carrying a four-point star on a staff. They sang carols and took up a collection for the church. It was customary at each house to treat them with food and drink.

Ebensee is noted for a bell-ringer tradition performed the night of January 5. Runners carry lighted translucent and highly decorated boxes on their heads, ringing large bells as they weave through the streets like a noisy conga line, supposedly scaring away any evil spirits. Next day comes commemoration of the Three Wise Men's arrival to marvel at the baby Jesus.

Finally, in an Austrian version of Mardi Gras, comes Fasching, a colorful and raucous final celebration just before the solemn onset of Lent. It involves a happy-go-lucky parade of citizens in rags and outlandish costumes with music and horseplay, culminating in the burning of a giant figure called the Fetzen beside

CHRISTMAS IN AUSTRIA 63

the Traun River. His passing denotes the passing of the holiday season.

The Austrians know how to keep Christmas, and it is nearly Easter before they turn it loose.

We are unlikely ever to repeat the Christmas journey. Long trips have become a physical challenge, and we wonder if we could handle the deep chill of the Austrian winter anymore. Nevertheless, we have always been glad we went back for that special Christmas. Many of its participants are gone. Ann is the last of her immediate family. Those who were children then have children of their own now. But as we gather our own family about us at Christmas time, we remember, and we are warmed by the memories.